Water in Watercolour

D1102483

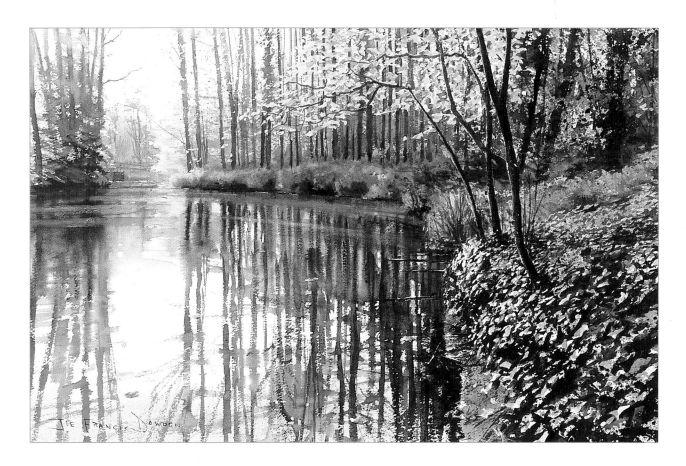

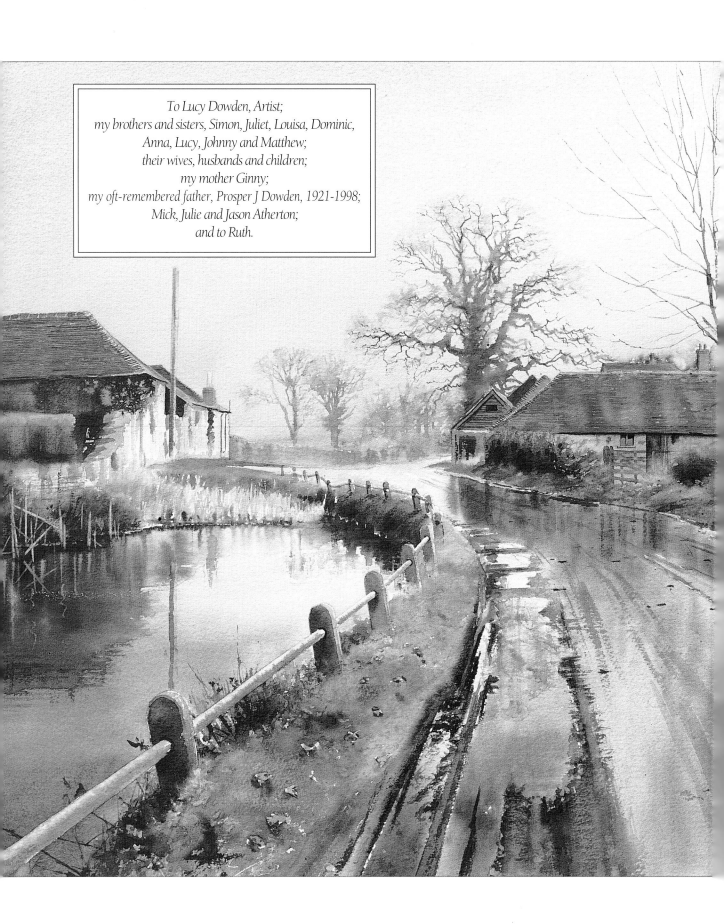

To Lucy Dowden, Artist;
my brothers and sisters, Simon, Juliet, Louisa, Dominic,
Anna, Lucy, Johnny and Matthew;
their wives, husbands and children;
my mother Ginny;
my oft-remembered father, Prosper J Dowden, 1921-1998;
Mick, Julie and Jason Atherton;
and to Ruth.

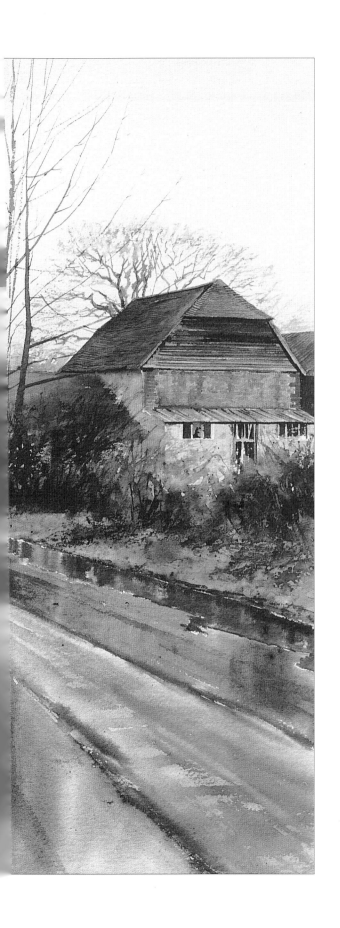

Water in
Watercolour

JOE FRANCIS
DOWDEN

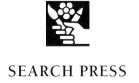

SEARCH PRESS

First published in Great Britain 2001

Search Press Limited
Wellwood, North Farm Road, Tunbridge Wells, Kent TN2 3DR

Reprinted 2002

Text copyright © Joe Francis Dowden 2001

Photographs © Search Press 2001, except the following:
pages 1, 6/7, 14–15, 26–29, 38 (bottom), 39, 46 (bottom), 47
and the front cover © Tim Piggins;
pages 2/3, 5 and 46 (top), © Jim Farrar;
inside front cover © Paul Bailey.

Design copyright © Search Press Ltd. 2001

ISBN: 0 85532 845 2

The publishers and author can accept no responsibility for any
consequences arising from the information, advice or instructions
given in this publication.

The publishers would like to thank Winsor & Newton for
supplying some the materials used in this book.

Suppliers
If you have difficulty in obtaining any of the materials and
equipment mentioned in this book, then please visit the Search
Press website for details of suppliers: www.searchpress.com

Alternatively, you can write to the Publishers at the address above,
for a current list of stockists, which includes firms who operate a
mail-order service, or you can write to Winsor & Newton
requesting a list of distributers.

Winsor & Newton, UK Marketing
Whitefriars Avenue, Harrow, Middlesex HA3 5RH

Publisher's note
All the step-by-step photographs in this book feature the
author, Joe Francis Dowden, demonstrating drawing
techniques. No models have been used.

There is reference to sable hair and other animal hair
brushes in this book. It is the publishers' custom to
recommend synthetic materials as substitutes for animal
products wherever possible. There is now a large number of
brushes available made from artificial fibres and they are
satisfactory substitutes for those made from natural fibres.

Colour separation by Croman. http://www.croman.es
Printed in Spain by A. G. Elkar S. Coop. 48180 Loiu (Bizkaia)

*I would like to thank Mike Reed, Bryan Robinson,
Helen and John Botting and Shirley and Jim Farrar for their help
and encouragement in my endeavours.
I am indebted to the farmers and rural craftsmen –
David and Robert Savage, Malcolm Sharp, Tony Reid, Doris
Campbell, Derek Ecton, Alice Purvis, Gerald Madgewick and
Nigel Bonham – who help maintain and nurture the landscape
that I paint, and to the Albury Estate and the Bray Estate.
I would also like to give special thanks to the
Lebus family, Andrew Street, Diane and Peter Jeorrett
and all my window-cleaning customers.*

Front cover
Morning River
*The dance of bright, rippled reflections in this river is captured
as sunshine lights the spring leaves from behind. Strong colour
is balanced by deep tones, an oft-repeated method in my
work. This scene shows that it is not only what you choose to
paint or how you paint it that matters, but also when you
paint it. Springtime brings fresh leaf colour, and sunshine
brings it all to life. As a rough guide, and this does depend on
the time of year, the best light is before 10.30 in the morning
and after 2.00 in the afternoon.*

Page 1
Journey's End
*In a few short miles, a glittering brook spills out of rural hills
to become a graceful river that then joins navigable water
heading for the sea. The gentle movement of long watery
reflections was achieved by first brushing zig-zag strokes of
water on to dry paper then, using rapid brush strokes, by
painting the reflections straight through the wet marks; the
colours have diffused along the lines of applied water to
produce the diverging reflections of the upper branches.*

Pages 2–3
Wet Wealden Landscape
*Puddles on a wet road and a pond – the whole countryside is
practically underwater! This painting is a good example of
how reflections are affected by the texture of the water surface.
The water in the puddles is still and smooth and reflects
hard-edged mirror images. However, the water on the road
takes on the texture of the tarmac so it reflects a more general
spread of light, less directly, to produce a sheen of soft-focus
images. Compare the sharp reflections of the large
background tree in the puddles with the soft reflections of the
nearer group of trees on the road. This difference can also be
seen where puddles mirror the pale sky above, but the road
next to them reflects a loose blue sheen.*

Contents

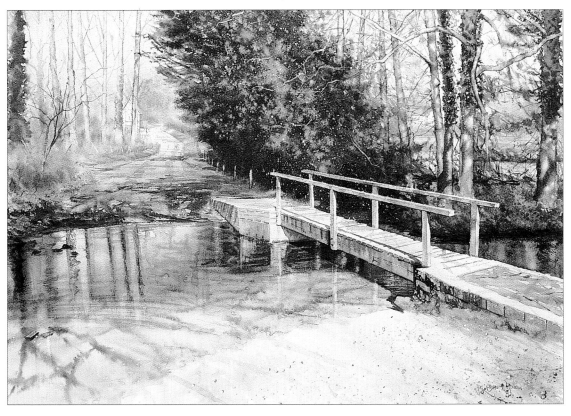

The Donkey Bridge
This bridge, a classic for children – and not a few adults – to play Pooh Sticks from, provides an ideal foil for this scene of two opposing flows of energy converging in the warm-toned shallow waters. It need not be difficult to let your wet washes work for you when blending colour to create the soft-focus tones on this river bed. These mainly comprise tree shadows painted with strong colours from the point of a brush. Harder-edged reflections were put in when these were dry, then the vertical bridge reflections were scuffed in with a slightly damp, stiff brush. This last move really puts the 'wet' in the wetness

Introduction

So, you would like to paint water that looks really wet? Watercolour is one of the best mediums for painting water and, in this book, I show you how I paint it. I have included the tricks, dodges, techniques (call them what you will) that I use to achieve realistic effects.

Remember that painting in watercolour is not an elitist sport, with a governing body ready to expel anyone not conforming to a set of rules. You can paint how you want, why you want, by whatever means you want, from whatever source material you want and with whatever equipment you have available – you make your own rules.

I have included step-by-step demonstrations for three types of water that you may come across: a deep, slow-moving river; a fast-moving stream; and a shallow stretch of still water. Visually, I have tried to capture every significant stage in the development of each painting, and I have kept the text as brief as possible.

Try painting the projects. Use them as guidelines to help you develop skills and to paint in your own unique way. Use the suggested set of colours or try your own and see what results you can achieve. Have fun!

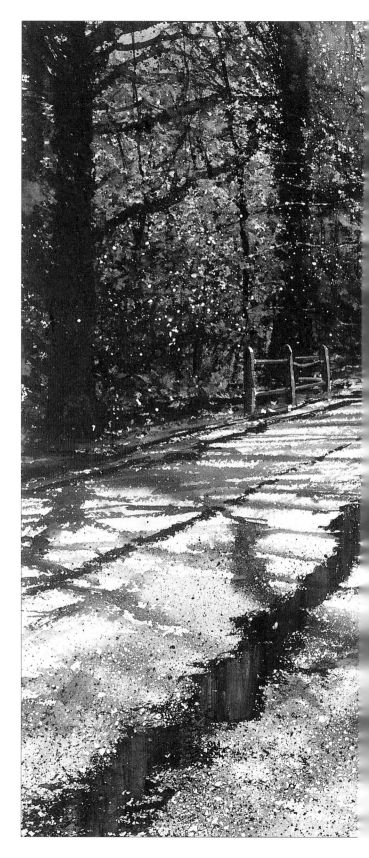

Passing Rainstorm

When a rainstorm marches across the countryside and leaves a brilliant, clear sky in its wake, the sun glints on a watery wonderland. A powerful tonal balance is required for such subjects, and this is achieved by splitting tones into extreme opposites and using very strong pigments.

Masking fluid spattered from a tooth brush has been used all over this painting; on both the bare paper and on top of some colours. For example, the fine, light, grainy texture on the road is created by spattering tiny spots of colours over spattered masking fluid. Larger spattered drops of masking fluid create the highlights on damp leaves glistening in the high overhead sun.

Gum arabic was painted into the puddles and the colour was brushed in vertically. Then, when the paint had dried, a damp bristle brush was scrubbed across them. The puddles would not look wet on their own: it is only the surrounding landscape – the trees, sky and the road – that make it look real!

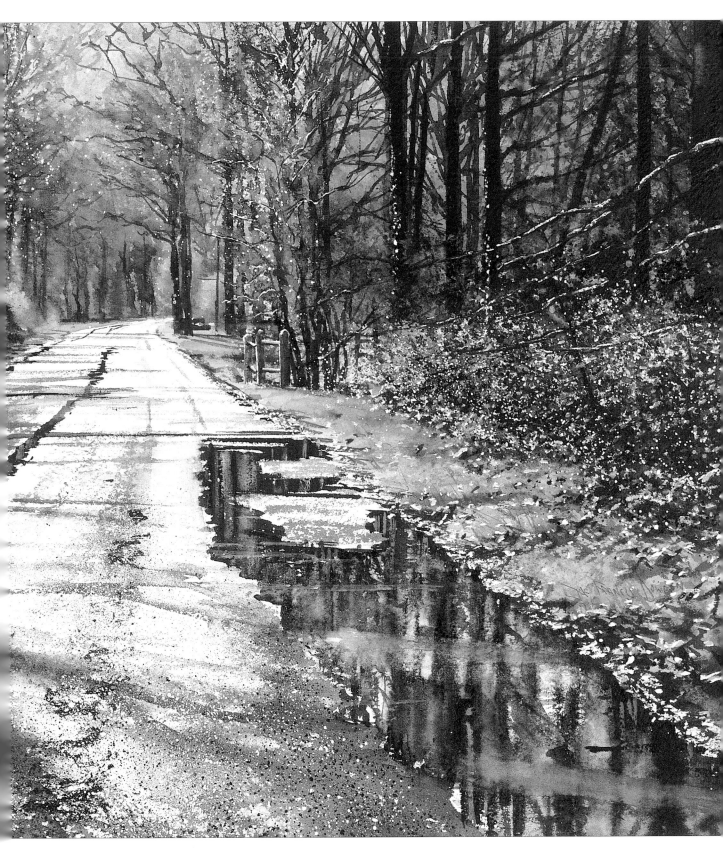

Materials

A pencil, some paper, brushes and a few colours – armed with these basics you can paint anything! For me, materials are part of the enjoyment of watercolour, not just a necessary evil, and having a few *extra* items in my armoury adds to the richness and fun of watercolour. A woodcock feather, a candle, a knife blade, a lump of brush-cleaning soap are just a few of the things I happily did without for years. Now they are old friends that add a personal touch to my work as well as making the act of painting more enjoyable !

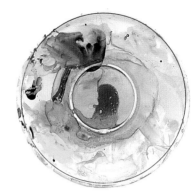

I use a variety of old plates and saucers for mixing colours.

Colours

I like to experiment with new colours and, currently, my paint box holds more than forty different tubes. I use them all on a regular basis, but not for one painting! I think it is a shame to spend one's life without ever trying the magnificent array of hues and pigments available. Why stick to a limited palette when you could be a millimetre away from discovery on the art shop shelf? Having lots of colours to choose from is no more expensive than having a limited palette – the greater the quantity, the less demand there is on each colour.

However, if you want to use a small palette of colours, great! Try using the first five colours in the list below and discover how many colours it is possible to mix from them. Then, you could add the next ten colours in the list. The other colours listed complete my most-used set of twenty-eight colours.

We all perceive colour slightly differently – there are no right and wrong choices – and our variations in taste and perception contribute to each of us being unique. I used specific colours to paint the step-by-step demonstrations in this book, but there is no reason why you cannot achieve very similar results with a more limited palette or different colours.

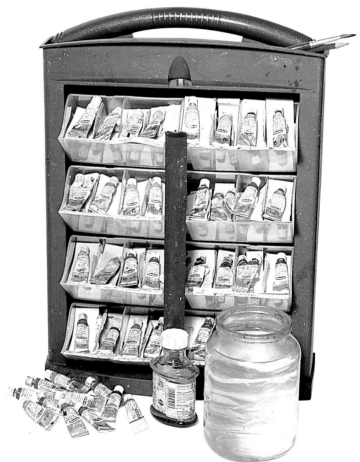

My paintbox of favourite colours

Phthalo blue, quinacridone red, cadmium lemon, burnt umber, ultramarine.

Cobalt blue, cobalt turquoise, phthalo green, Naples yellow, yellow ochre, cadmium red, light red , burnt sienna, Payne's gray, titanium white.

Indigo, cerulean blue, helio turquoise, olive green, Winsor emerald, cadmium yellow pale, cadmium orange, Winsor red, alizarin crimson, Pozzuoli earth, Venetian red , raw sienna , Chinese white.

Each colour has particular characteristics – transparency/opacity, texture, ability to flow or stay put, light-fastness and brightness. For example, I use Naples yellow not only for its colour, but for its covering power, its subtlety, its soft texture (like cream), and its power to influence other colours. It can be used as a medium to build into, putting it down as an initial wash, then working other colours in, and it works equally well for skies and rivers. These characteristics vary from range to range and depend on many factors, the most notable of which are the quality and strength of the pigments and binder (gum arabic) used to make them.

I also use gum arabic as a retarding medium in many of my water paintings. It is brilliant for certain types of reflections, as it slows the movement of pigment through a wash, stopping it travelling and changing shape or diffusing into the surrounding area. When the wash dries the reflected images are realistically blurred. All you have to do is to apply the gum arabic, paint into it, then let the gum work for you. Use it sparingly or it will be too thick to paint into, and it could even dry as a thick, hard sheen.

If you feel intimidated by the variety on offer, remember that nobody knows all the millions of possible combinations and their applications. Each colour is a little jewel, a potential building block in your work, so make choosing them part of the pleasure of watercolour.

Brushes

Even if your work is excellent, top-quality brushes could improve your painting skills. I find sable brushes are best – their hairs return easily to a point, they hold a good quantity of colour and they have the capacity to release it steadily. Less expensive, synthetic and synthetic/sable mixed-fibres brushes are catching up; they can do a large amount of the work and point well, and I have used them extensively even though they do not perfectly mimic the qualities of sable. However, they do not clean as quickly as sable, so take this into account when changing colours while working rapidly.

I choose brushes for the character of the marks they make and then allow them to make those marks; to speak for themselves. If I had to start from scratch with a limited budget, I would buy one top-quality No 2 or No. 3 round brush, one mid-range No. 6 round, one No. 16 goat or squirrel hair wash brush, and two or three synthetic round brushes between No. 4 and No. 12.

Try to avoid mixing paint with your best sable brushes. Wash brushes gently in cold water. You could use a little vegetable-based, artists' brush-cleaning soap. Never use ordinary soap or detergent.

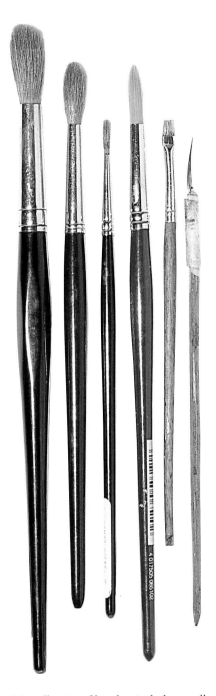

My collection of brushes includes small bristle brushes for scrubbing out colour, and a tiny woodcock pinfeather, taped to a wooden handle, which I use instead of a rigger brush for fine detail work.

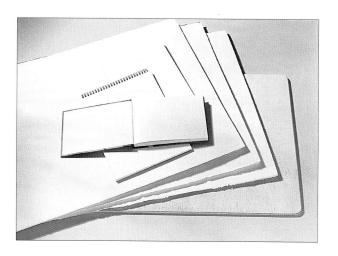

Paper

The surface texture, or tooth, of watercolour papers ranges from the smoothness of typing paper to almost the roughness of masonry. There are three basic finishes – Hot Pressed, Not (or Cold Pressed) and Rough – but the degree of smoothness varies from brand to brand.

Hot Pressed papers have a very smooth surface that is created during manufacture by passing the paper through heated rollers. I use this paper for atmospheric paintings of evening light and marine scenes, and for line and wash work, but I have not used it for any of the paintings in this book.

The term 'Not' refers to the fact that the paper is not hot pressed. These papers have a slightly textured surface which is created by passing the paper between felts or mats which are fed through cold rollers. The texture of this type of paper is quite subtle – it does not leave its 'signature' in a painting – and I use it for most of my river paintings.

Rough papers are not pressed at all, and the texture can be very rough, especially on some heavier papers. This type of paper is very versatile. You can work wet into wet to create a smooth sky wash, or you can use a dry brush to create wonderful textures – ripples on water, tree bark, foliage, grass – the possibilities are endless.

Watercolour paper is available in different thicknesses or weights. A 200gsm (90lb) paper is quite thin and light, while a 640gsm (300lb) paper is very heavy and thick.

The whiteness of paper varies, and I often use the whiteness of lighter-toned papers to create brightness. Mellow-toned papers also show colour brightly and, visually, highlights saved on a strong watercolour painting will read as white.

Papers also come in varying degrees of hardness. Soft papers are sensitive and can be used for building up subtle textures, but they may rip when masking fluid is removed. However, such tearing can enhance the final image, as with jagged sky holes in woodland. A hard paper can take any amount of masking fluid without ripping.

I used a soft, 425gsm (200lb), white cotton rag Not paper for many of the paintings in this book, but do try out different types and brands of paper. It is fascinating to see the results.

Stretching tools

I stretch all my paper, even the heavy paper I use for the biggest paintings. I soak it thoroughly, lay it on a painting board for a few minutes to let it carry on expanding, then staple it along its edges. I keep the staples close together, especially on lighter weight papers, and slightly in from the edge of the sheet – if they are too near the edge the paper may rip. As it dries, the paper shrinks and becomes very taut. I cut the finished painting off the board, then use a tack lifter and a pair of pliers to remove the staples.

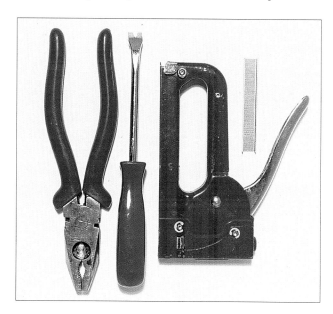

Resists

I use masking fluid to save whites. Use it with care as it tends to lift underlying colour and it can rip soft papers when it is removed. It wrecks brushes, so use old or cheap brushes or colour shapers to apply it. For random spattering use an old tooth-brush – create a fine spray of tiny dots by dragging the thumb across the bristles, or make larger drop-lets by banging the brush down against your hand. Clean all tools in a hot water. Comb the bristles of toothbrushes with a needle to remove dried fluid.

I also use candle wax to create texture, rubbing it straight on to either the bare paper or on top of a dried wash prior to overpainting.

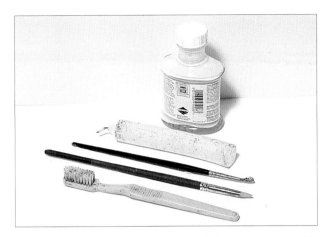

Masking fluid and candle wax are useful resists. Use an old brush, colour shaper or a toothbrush to apply the masking fluid. Rub the candle straight on to the paper.

Other equipment

Hairdryer This is an essential tool for my studio work, saving hours of waiting for the paper to dry naturally. Do not dry your paper too rapidly, and dry work evenly to avoid back-runs and hard edges.

Craft knife For making marks on a painting such as sparkles in water; for cutting masks; or for use with masking fluid to rip up parts of an image and reveal white paper.

Scissors For cutting masks, stencils, and paper.

Masking Tape I usually stick strips this of round the aperture shapes of paintings. I also use it as a resist and to make masks.

Scrap paper I rip up pieces of this to create masks for spattering colour. The natural-looking torn edge works well for the edge of a river bank. Sometimes, I cut masks in the shape of a tree branch, for example, then use this to scrub out colour.

Tracing paper I use this to transfer my sketches on to watercolour paper.

Paper towel For dabbing off excess colour. Use it wet or dry to create clouds in wet skies, and for other effects. Twist it up into coils for mare's-tail clouds.

Pencil I use B grade pencils for most of my work.

Artists' brush-cleaning soap Use this with cold water to clean brushes.

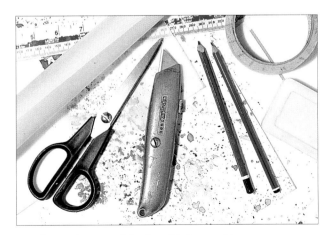

I have two powerful hairdryers (one is a spare) to dry my work and, sometimes, I use them both at once!

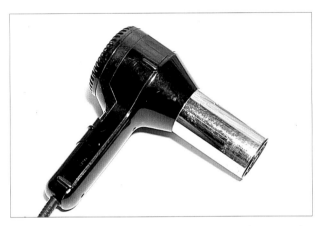

Pencils, a ruler, a craft knife or blades, masking tape, scrap paper, tracing paper, paper towel and artists' brush-cleaning soap complete my essential set of equipment.

Composition

Composition is the art of apportioning space in a satisfying and truthful way – for me, it is the architecture of art.

A simple approach is to place a frame or aperture round your chosen image, rather than trying to arrange individual elements within a frame. Then, by moving the frame about, you can control the composition.

Find a focal point and move the frame to make this point slightly off-centre. The focal point can be distant, out of focus or even indefinable, so that the eye wanders and explores the whole composition, never arriving at the 'end' of the painting. River scenes have a ready-made passage to lead the eye to the focal point.

Decide on where to place the horizon. A high horizon gives a painting more foreground, creating depth and enhancing distance, whereas a low horizon gives a sense of space and height, and a tall sky can be used for painting wide expanses of open country. The horizon might define a long narrow rectangle of sky area above it, and a much broader one below – two simple counterbalancing shapes. A composition can be that simple.

Opposite

This comfortable composition places the viewer on the river bank. The wide expanse of water gives ample space for wonderful reflections. The main group of trees is well to the right of centre and the focal point is just beyond them. The footpath leads us into the picture, then the other elements of the painting take over making the eye wander all over it. The small white-roofed building, also set off-centre, provides contrast for the gentle wall of foliage in the distance. Its image also contributes to the reflections on the surface of the river.

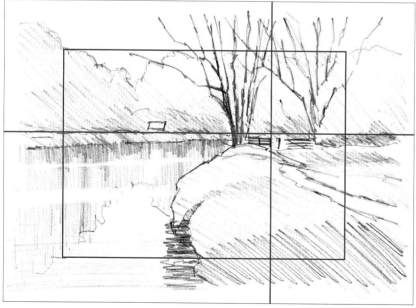

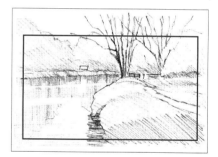

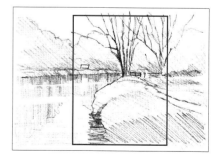

This is one of my sketches of the scene depicted in the two paintings opposite. I have superimposed the frame that I used for the top painting and marked the horizon and the main focal point (where the vertical line crosses the horizon).

The horizon is well off centre creating two rectangles – a narrow one for the background and a larger one for the foreground. The foreground area is made up of several triangular shapes all converging at the focal point. The two groups of trees form inverted triangles that link the two rectangles.

Experiment with different shapes and sizes of frame. Let the composition dictate the proportions of your painting, not the size of paper you are using.

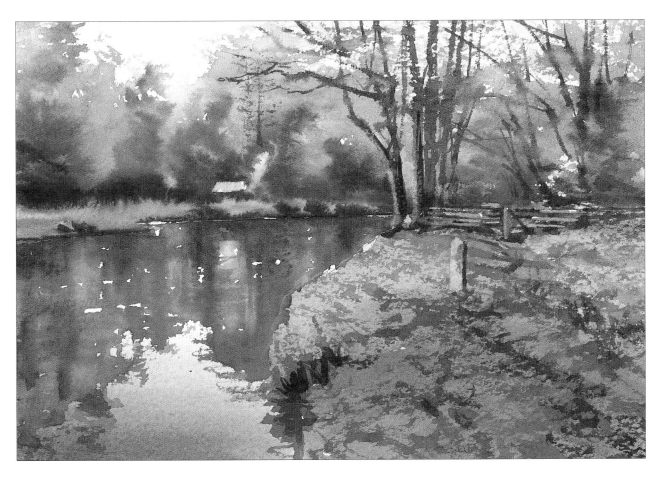

This painting is the same scene as that above, but from a different viewpoint. We are much closer to the trees which are now just left of centre. The river and path both lead us to an indistinct focal point above the fence and gate. The building, now with a red roof to provide a point of interest, counters all the greens. The high horizon creates a deep foreground area, the perspective of which is enhanced by the leaf details at the bottom of the painting.

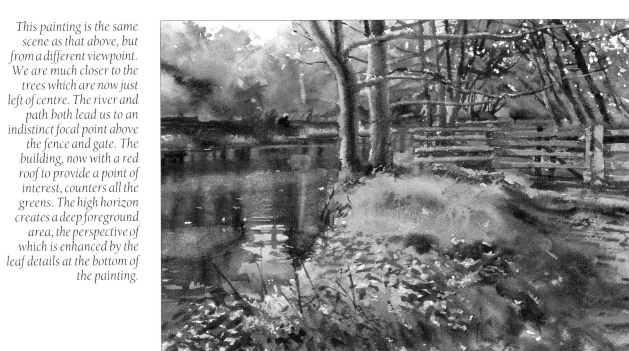

Using colour

The colours of water are taken from the surrounding areas, and in landscapes these are the colours of the sky and foliage. For water to look wet, the other elements of the landscape must be well executed, so I take as much care of these as I do for the water itself.

I use three categories of colour for my paintings – bright, brown and dark. Strong bright colours, orange, green, red, blue and yellow can be used to mix any colour. The vital browns or earth colours – burnt sienna, burnt umber, Naples yellow and others – make subtle shades. To help get intense darks I use indigo and Payne's Gray.

I like painting back-lit scenes drenched with strong bright colours, and there is no brighter yellow than that of spring leaves with a low sun shining through them from behind. For this, try using cadmium lemon, with a little burnt sienna and a tiny bit of any green. Some people find it difficult to mix green. There is no problem if you really use your eyes – look at how a 'green' is affected by light, and see how many separate colours there are. A great guideline is to start with a yellow, add a little green or blue, then warm it with a brown. Mix other greens using different blues and greens with the yellow.

I work fast and I try to keep my water colours wet for as long as possible. I mix plenty of colour right at the start – you do not have much time to go back and mix more.

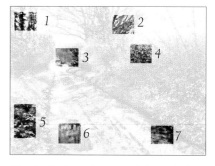

Key to the boxed areas of the painting shown below and opposite.

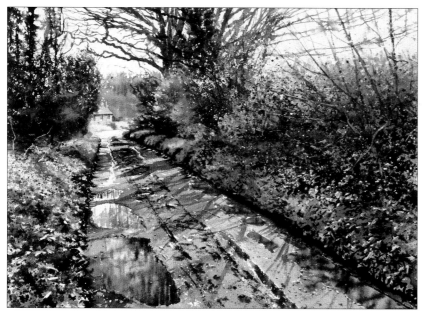

This painting of a wet lane deep in the countryside, a simple but great subject, embraces most of the techniques used in this book. I have given brief explanations of how I used them on these pages.

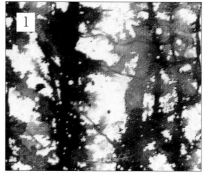

I spattered masking fluid with a toothbrush and left it to dry. I crisscrossed water over the area with the point of a brush, leaving plenty of dry paper. I then painted the tree trunks and branches across these wet marks using dark mixes of phthalo green and alizarin crimson, with touches of cadmium lemon. The paint diffuses in the wet areas and stays defined on the dry parts. Removing the masking fluid reveals sky holes.

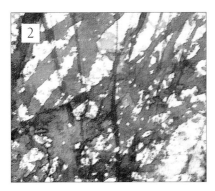

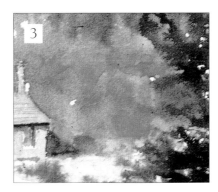

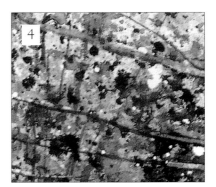

This area, which has the sun glaring from the right-hand side, was painted in much the same way as area 1, but with paler colours (mixes of burnt umber) and thicker branches.

For this soft foliage, behind the cottage, I used the point of a brush to drop ultramarine and burnt umber into a wet wash of Naples yellow with touches of cadmium lemon and burnt sienna.

I started this area of leafy foliage by spattering a small amount of masking fluid to create highlights. I then built up the colour, layer by layer, working from pale tones of cadmium lemon, through a range of mid and dark greens to the dark of indigo. For each layer, I spattered water, spattered colour into the water then left that colour to dry. I used a blade to scratch out the tops of branches, painted their under parts with darks, then extended some of these marks by scrubbing with a dampened small stiff brush.

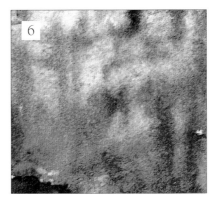

I used a colour shaper to mask the large highlights on these foreground leaves. I then used the spattering techniques and colours mentioned for area 4 to build up the colour. Finally, when the masking fluid had been removed, I touched in parts of the leaves with greens, then used indigo with the point of a brush to define a few very dark leaves carefully.

I soaked the area of this puddle, brushed in gum arabic and laid a wash of phthalo blue. Then, working wet into wet, I dropped in vertical bands of darker colours taken from the surrounding landscape.

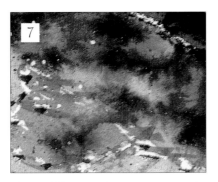

This puddle started out as a wet wash of Naples yellow. I crisscrossed several darks, wet into wet, then dabbed in touches of cadmium lemon.

Correcting mistakes

I made a complete mess of the large puddle in the foreground of this painting (area 6), so I used the adhesive quality of masking fluid to 'delete' it, then painted it once again.

First, I used a very sharp blade to cut a shallow incision round the outline of the puddle. I then applied a thick layer of masking fluid over the whole area. When the masking fluid was completely dry, I used the tip of the blade to rip a corner of the paper under the masking fluid. Then, still using the blade, I carefully peeled off the masking fluid and a very thin layer of paper. This method only works with soft watercolour papers.

Types of water

I have two basic tips for painting water: keep it wet and blurred; and keep all reflections vertical. By and large these practices will make any water scenes ring true, but there are many different kinds of water, and there are watercolour techniques to make them look real and wet!

We all know that, on its own, water is completely transparent. However, in nature, water takes up (reflects) colours from the sky, foliage and objects around it, and, to make the water look wet, the painting of these is just as important as the painting of the water.

The sketches on these pages, the step-by-step demonstrations and the gallery of finished paintings illustrate just a few of the multitude of watery scenes about us. I hope you will find them useful and that they will inspire you to paint your favourite stretch of water.

Remember that water bends, refracts and reflects light – twisting, breaking and diffusing shapes – and recreating these characteristics in watercolour is our exciting challenge.

Autumn River

In this peaceful river scene, the soft reflections on the far side of the river were worked wet into wet, with colour brushed in vertically. While these were still wet horizontal ripples were dragged across them. The reflections of the boat and the foreground ripples were painted wet on dry.

The dark tones of the barge and the far river bank contrast well with the strong red stripes and the warm, lighter tones in the rest of the painting.

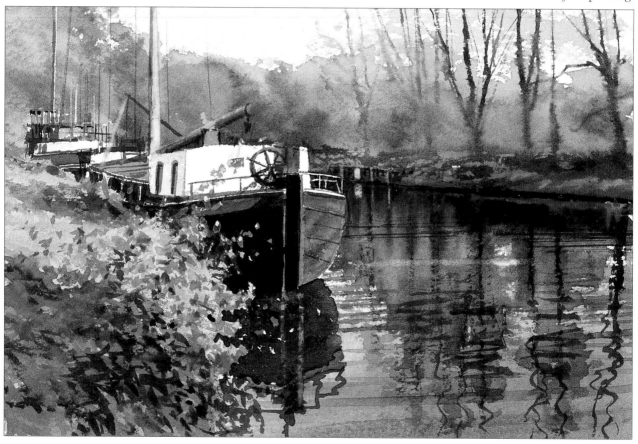

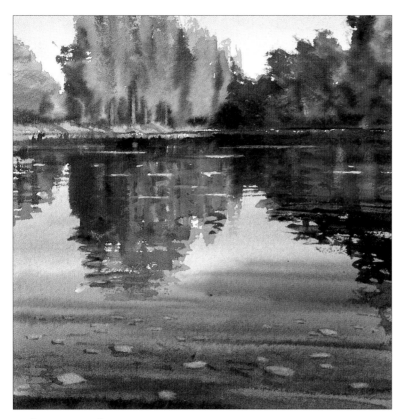

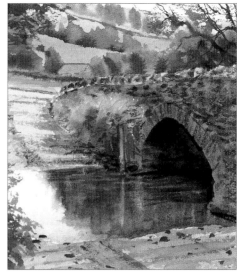

Rural Ford

The reflections in this shallow stream, soft and blurred, but with a slightly hard edge, were worked entirely wet into wet. When the reflections were dry, the pale vertical marks were leached out with a dampened stiff brush, then dabbed with paper towel to stop hard edges forming.

Midsummer Lake

I started the water of this shallow lake by laying in some streaks of masking fluid to indicate clumps of weed floating on the surface. I then painted an upside-down sky, working from the bottom upwards. When this was dry, the tree reflections were painted with very strong colours, wet into wet, then vertical ripples and streaks of a semi-opaque yellow were added. The stones in the foreground were leached out with a dampened stiff brush (see page 44).

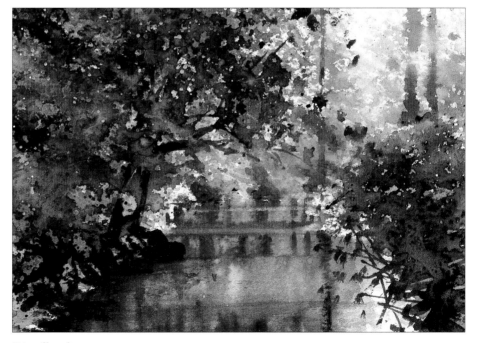

Woodland stream

In shallow woodland streams the reflection of the tree canopy allows the river bottom to become visible. Streaks of sunlight run across the river bed, and patchy sky reflections from the tree tops show as vertical light patches, blurred in the water.

Deep water

For my first step-by-step project, I have chosen an autumnal scene of a deep, slow-moving river. If a river is to look convincing, it has to sit comfortably in the surrounding landscape, and the challenge in this composition, where there is hardly any sky, is to merge the old bridge and wooded backdrop, and set the scene for their reflections to be painted in the river. The solution is to mask around the arches and along the parapet, leaving you free to concentrate on the background. Dynamic brush strokes can then be used to paint the trees, and you can work right up to the bridge itself, without fear of painting over it. The wooded hillside in the background helps push the bridge forward to create a three-dimensional scene that looks real.

The river is painted with simple washes with a little fine tuning to give it depth. Gum arabic is incredibly effective for creating a wet look and for making reflections blurred and realistic. Note that the reflections are not entirely symmetrical with the objects they mirror, and the movement on the surface, slight as it is, softens their edges. The colours and tones I use for water are often stronger than those of the objects they reflect, but here I have moderated them. For me there are no rules to be applied every time, just principles and guidelines to build confidence.

I used 425gsm (200lb) Not paper, and the finished painting measures 430 x 295mm (17 x 11½in).

You will need

Burnt sienna, burnt umber, cadmium lemon, cadmium orange, cobalt blue, cobalt turquoise, Naples yellow, Payne's gray, phthalo blue, phthalo green, quinacridone red, ultramarine, Venetian red

Candle, gum arabic, masking fluid

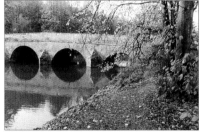

Reference photograph.

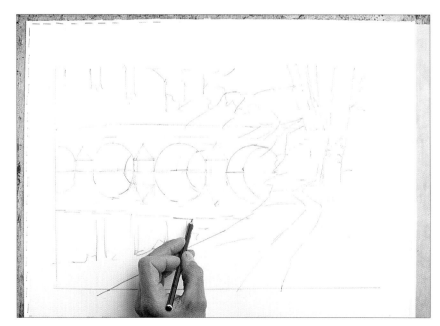

1. Sketch the subject on tracing paper then transfer the basic outlines on to the watercolour paper.

2. Use strips of masking tape to mark the chosen aperture shape. Lightly sketch in a few leaves on the foreground bank of the river – make some large, some medium-sized and some small – then sketch in some more on the overhanging branches. Use an old brush to apply masking fluid randomly over these leaves, then mask a few more leaves floating on the water.

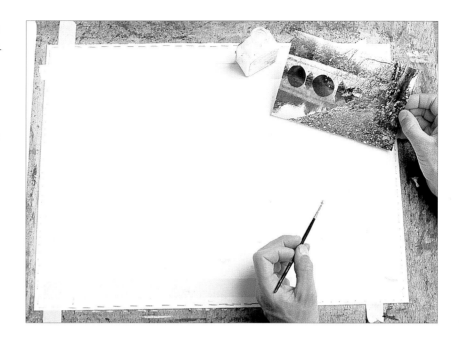

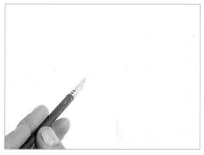

3. Use a colour shaper to apply more masking fluid along the parapet of the bridge and round the right-hand side of the arches. Leave the masking fluid to dry, or speed up the process with a hairdryer.

4. Working at the top right-hand corner of the picture, use roughly torn pieces of scrap paper to mask out the sky, the bridge, the river, the foreground river bank and the tree trunks.

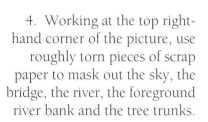

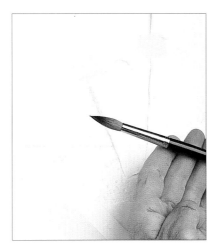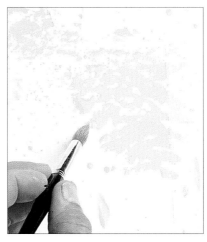

5. Splatter water over the exposed area of the paper.

6. Mix cadmium lemon with a touch of Naples yellow, then spatter this colour randomly over the exposed area of paper.

7. Carefully spread some of the spattered yellow to form larger patches of colour.

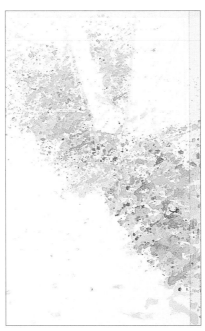

Judging hue and tone

If you cut a small aperture in a piece of white paper and place it over your painted image (left), you isolate an area of colour. The contrast between it and the neutral white of the paper will help you evaluate hue and tone more easily.

A photograph can provide a useful reference. If you use one, place the aperture over the corresponding part of it (right), and compare it to your painted image. The idea is not slavishly to copy the photographic image, but to experiment and see how to strengthen your work.

I use this method with photographs, tonal sketches and watercolours painted on site. Remember that none of these reference sources are 'correct', but you can use them to help improve your work.

8. Remove the paper mask. Add a touch of burnt sienna to the yellow, then spatter across the top centre part of the previous marks. Again, use the brush to spread some of this colour, then leave to dry. Apply masking fluid down the lightest side of the tree trunks, then leave this to dry.

9. Replace the paper mask, then spatter more water over the exposed area. Strengthen the yellow with phthalo green and more burnt sienna, then spatter this over the previous colours. Introduce burnt umber to the palette, then repeat the spattering technique using various greens.

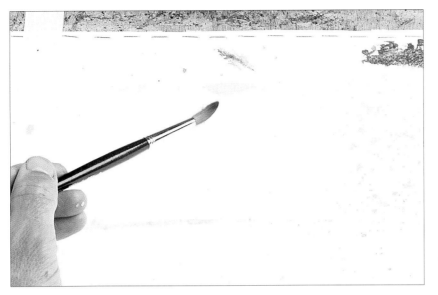

10. Use a dry brush to apply water to the tree tops above the bridge. Gently sweep the brush from side to side so that water sits on the texture of paper. Feather this water into the dry sky area.

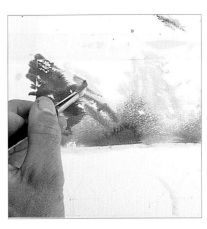

11. Working quickly, wet into wet, start to build up the colours, of the foliage. This area needs to be quite dark, so use intense colour mixes of Naples yellow, cadmium lemon, burnt sienna, and cobalt blue.

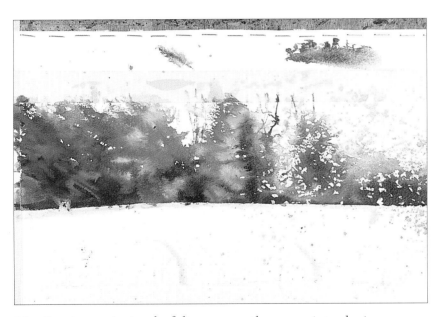

12. Continue painting the foliage across the paper, introducing ultramarine, quinacridone red and cadmium orange to create other tones of green and yellows.

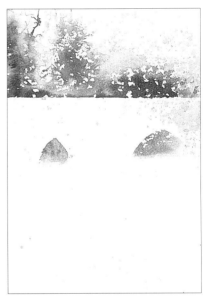

13. Use mixes of cadmium lemon, ultramarine and burnt umber, wet into wet, to paint the areas of foliage that are visible through the arches of the bridge.

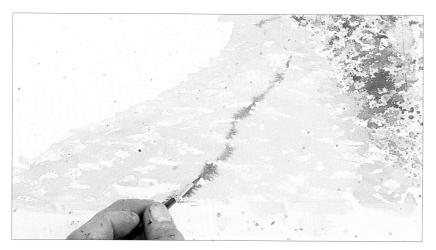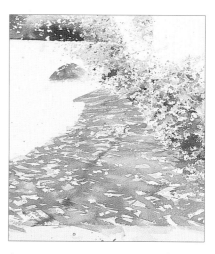

14. Spatter water over the right-hand foliage below the trees, then spatter this area with bright greens – mixes of cadmium yellow and phthalo green with touches of burnt umber and cobalt turquoise. Leave to dry. Mix a brown from Venetian red with touches phthalo green and cadmium lemon. Mix cadmium lemon and Naples yellow, add a touch of the brown mix, then, using crisscross brush strokes, paint the foreground river bank. While this colour is still wet, use one of the green mixes to add a shadow to define the edge of the footpath. Leave to dry.

15. Crisscross water over the foreground, then apply the brown mix with similar brush strokes. Make large strokes at the bottom, then gradually make finer strokes as you work up the paper. Add touches of the yellow mix, wet into wet, then leave to dry.

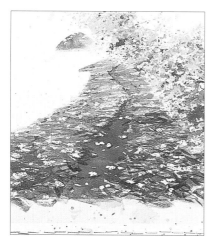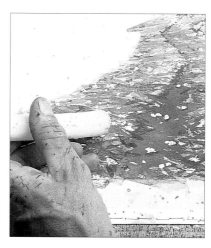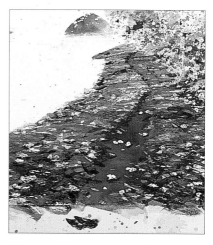

16. Add a touch of ultramarine to the brown mix. Crisscross water over the foreground, then work dark tones selectively over the area, building up the layers of fallen leaves and adding shape to the footpath. Use a dry brush to obscure the crispness of the previous brush strokes and to mimic the untidiness of leaves.

17. Rub candle wax selectively over the foreground area . . .

18. . . . then use Payne's gray to work really dark tones on top of the previous colours, especially over the waxed areas. Re-define the shadow on the footpath.

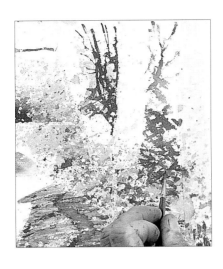

19. Use Payne's gray to paint the branches and foliage behind the tree trunks.

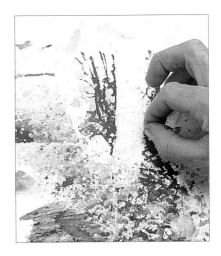

20. Remove the masking fluid from tree trunks and parapet. Reinstate the small areas of masking fluid for the leaves that break the line of the parapet.

21. Mix a grey from cobalt blue and Naples yellow, then lay a wash of this colour across the bridge. Leave to dry. Create warm and cool tones of grey by adding touches burnt sienna and ultramarine respectively, then use a semi-dry brush to add tone, texture and shape to the bridge.

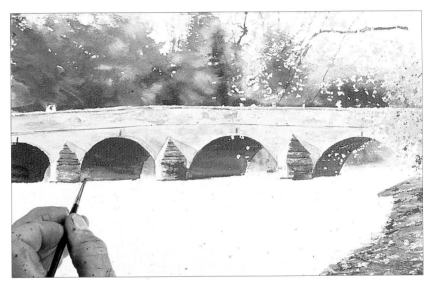

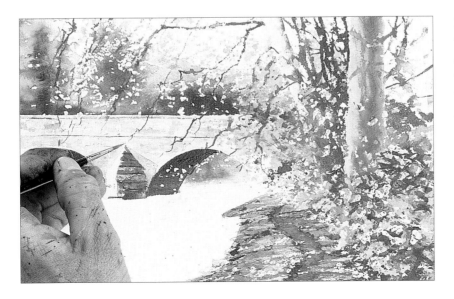

22. Mix a light greyish brown with Naples yellow and a touch of cobalt blue, then paint the tree trunks. Add more cobalt blue on the shadowed side of the trunks and a little yellow green (phthalo green and cadmium lemon) on the light side. Build up a three-dimensional effect by adding touches of Payne's gray, wet into wet, on the dark shadow and the shadows of the branches that cross the trunk. Use Payne's gray to add fine branches that hang down across the bridge.

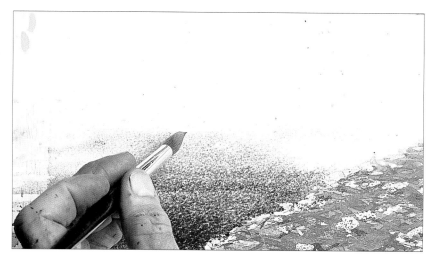

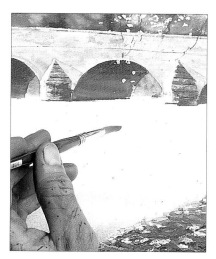

23. Now start to work on the river. First, mix a pale grey sky colour using Payne's gray and phthalo blue. Wet the area up to the edge of the bridge reflection with water, then apply a gradated wash, diluting the colour as you work up the paper. Use this wash to define the edge of the river bank. Leave to dry.

24. Wet the reflection of the bridge, then brush gum arabic into this area to slow the spread of colour in the next stage.

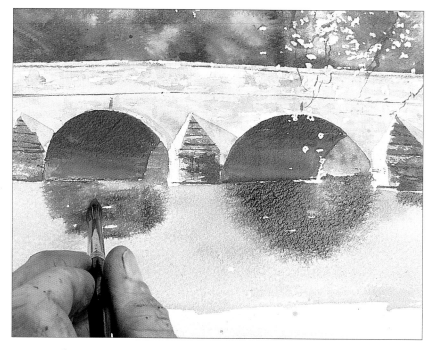

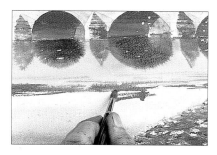

26. Lay horizontal strokes of colour into the wet wash to create rippled reflections from the trees above the bridge. Continue these ripples downwards, wet on dry with lots of water . . .

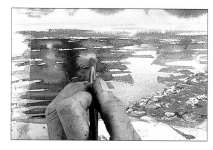

25. Mix burnt sienna, cobalt blue and Naples yellow, then paint in the reflection of the bridge. While the paint is still wet, start to work the reflections of the arches using mixes of Payne's grey and burnt umber. Use more of the same colour to define the masonry line along the reflection of the parapet. Notice how the gum arabic stabilises the soft-focus effect of the arch reflections; the pigments tend to stay where they are and not blend into the surrounding colour.

27. . . .then work vertical bands of cadmium lemon and Payne's gray wet-into-wet.

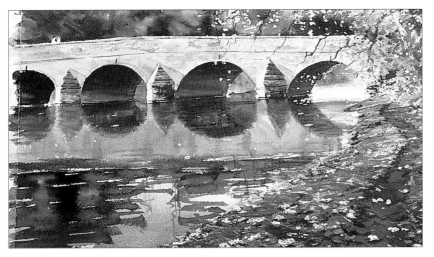

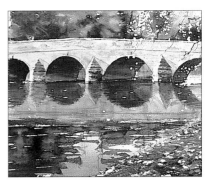

28. Go back to the reflection of the bridge and make short vertical brush strokes with a darker mix (add a touch of phthalo green). Rework the darks under the arches then add touches of cadmium lemon.

29. Remove all masking fluid, then use cadmium red light and ultramarine to add two figures on the bridge. Add fine, dark horizontal strokes across the bottom of bridge's reflection. Leave to dry.

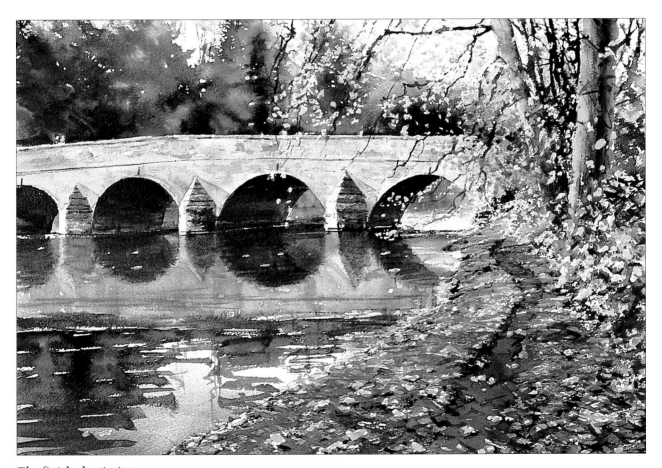

The finished painting.

After removing all the masking fluid, I decided to touch in most of the white leaves with neat cadmium yellow and touches of burnt sienna.

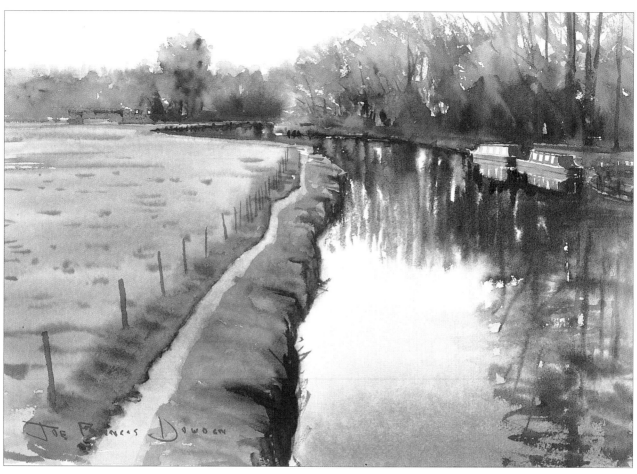

River Navigation

In this rapid sketch, viewed from a bridge across the river, the surface of the water picks up the deep tones from the sky. Rough brush strokes were used to indicate the wooded areas on the river banks. Neat colours, straight from the tube, were painted wet into wet to create the distant trees. The river was worked wet, but I left a few flashes of dry paper as highlights and for the reflections of the boats which were worked when the main stretch of water was dry.

The Old Mill

This sketch was painted in the heat of summer, and the colours seemed to dry as soon as I laid them down. I worked fast and loose with plenty of strong colours. I used a small stiff brush to scrub some streaks across the mill pond to indicate slight ripples on the surface of the water.

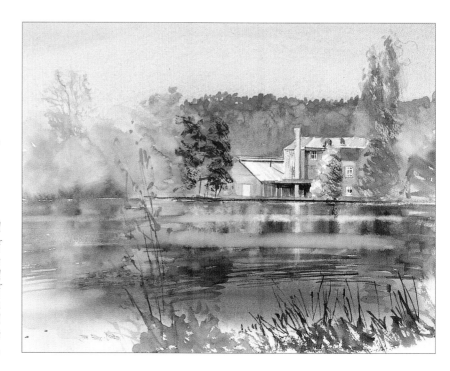

26

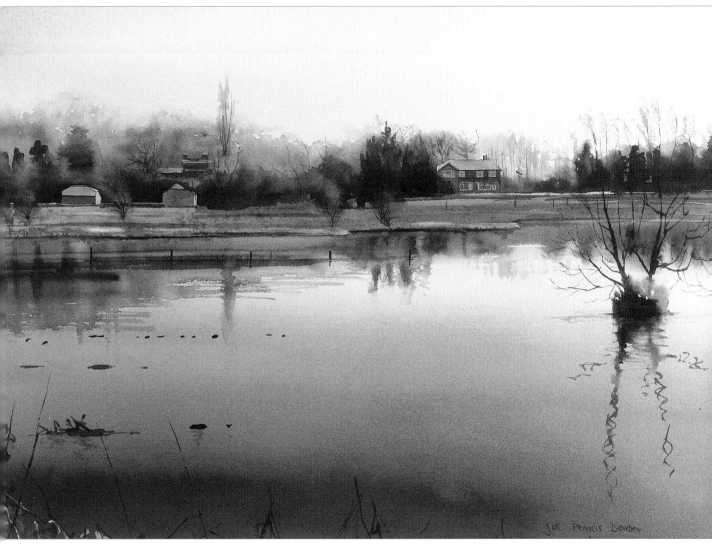

New Day Rising

Early morning light ignites this misty horizon. The view is looking eastwards and the rising sun, lighting up the foggy breath of morning, is beginning to flood through the veil of woodland. The right-hand side of the scene is the nearest to the light source, so the sky is lighter here than at the left.

To achieve the geography of light in this painting, I painted a wash, down and across the paper, working from the top left-hand corner where the sky is darkest. The reflection of the sky, mirrored in the still water, picks up darker tones from the sky that is above and out of the image, as well as the dark tone of the mud on the bed of the lake. I started this stretch of water with a gradated wash of burnt sienna, working from the far bank down the middle of the water. I then mixed a black

wash, made from phthalo blue, crimson alizarin and burnt umber, and worked this up from the bottom of the painting. While this was still wet, I returned to the foreground and applied more colour until it was very dark.

Notice that none of the objects is near the centre of the composition, and that none is strong enough to interfere with the tranquil mood. The tall, thin poplar consists of a few streaks of colour painted into a brush stroke of water, and the reflection is almost identical. The reflections of the branches of the half-submerged willow are just two wavy lines. Doubling a reflection in this way captures the movement of a brief instant in time – very effective for thin objects.

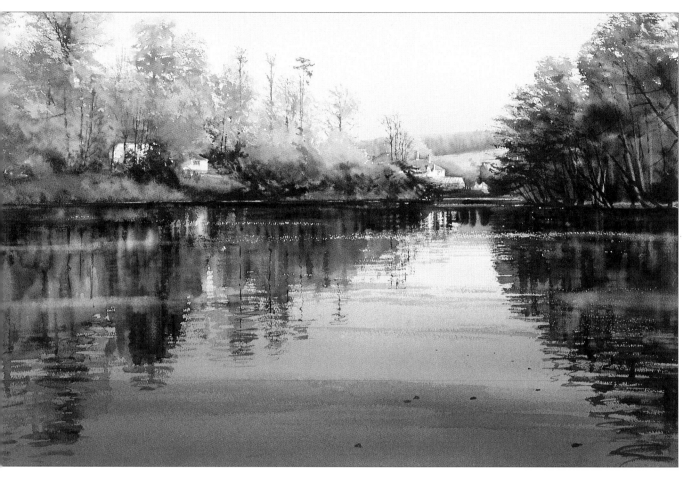

Vale end

This ragged autumn woodland glows in the evening sunshine as the warm light from the setting sun bathes the lakeside forest from a low angle. Orange tones contrast with the darks in the dense shadows and the deep blue of the water. How do you paint this scene? The key is to start with a soft grey across the sky, taking it down, but not too far, into the top of the woodland. This grey will appear quite pale when the other colours are put in, but it will still be dark enough to enhance the whites and warm lights. Note how the whites of the cottage and house in the distance create small centres of interest.

Warm browns – burnt sienna mixed with cadmium orange, cadmium yellow and light red, Venetian red or Pozzuoli earth – contribute to the transparent underglazing of the woodland. I used a 640gsm (300lb) rough paper for this painting so that when the darker browns (burnt umber mixed with ultramarine) were applied with a dry brush, the surface texture produced the ragged form of autumn leaves. The trees on the right-hand side were painted with much darker tones, using both wet-into-wet and dry brush techniques.

The water is a simple upside-down sky, painted initially with a gradated wash of Phthalo blue and indigo, strengthened with burnt umber and alizarin crimson in the foreground. When this was dry, I rubbed a candle across the water.

The reflections were worked very wet, with many colours and tones and, to accentuate the perspective, I made the horizontal ripples broader and more widely spaced as they come forward. Note how the candle wax has left an attractive highlight that indicates the wake of a waterfowl or a breath of wind ruffling the surface of the water.

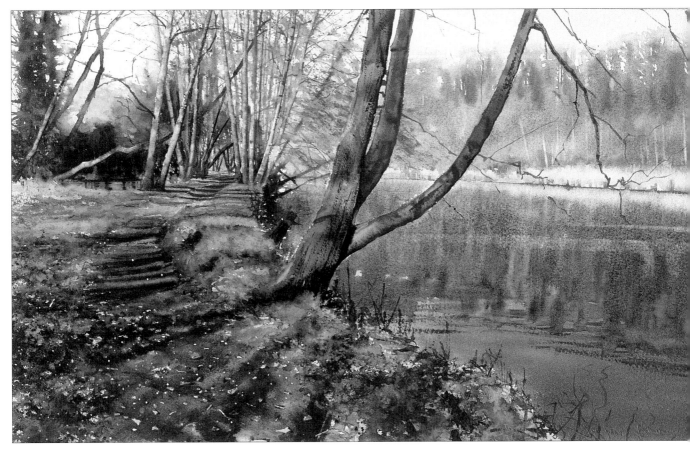

Deep Waters

This stretch of water is the same as that featured opposite and on page 48. These three paintings demonstrate how the same location can appear completely different, simply by changing the time of day, the season of the year or by moving the viewpoint.

The horizon, high above the centre line of the composition, accentuates the foreground area, and the converging angles of the footpath, the areas of grass and the distant bank create depth and perspective.

The footpath leads the eye into the picture, but the indefinable focal point allows the eye to wander over the whole painting. The leaning trees take you across the two halves of the painting, each of which could make a composition on its own. Looking across the lake, we take in the distant hillside but the

vertical marks in the water bring us down to the area where the reflections start to break up and lead us back to the foreground. For me, this painting makes the eye work – creating movement in the landscape – the viewer is placed in the landscape and given the choice of which way to look.

With two scenes in one, we can see there are no rules to composition. Just a few basic guidelines are often all you need to help you frame the scene and decide how to construct it. Keeping the horizon and the focal point off-centre, and using elements such as the footpath and trees to lead the eye through the painting, helped me to construct this scene. You do not always have to keep to guidelines – there are no rules – just experiment and see what you can do.

Lively water

In this next demonstration I show you how I deal with moving water, and I have chosen this view of a river that tumbles through the countryside, rushing down a succession of fast-flowing reaches.

The natural fibres of brushes, used in a loose rhythmic way, release the energy for waves on its lively surface. Bright colour is balanced with dark tone. Halation reveals the power of the sun and all the elements are reflected on the river's shining course.

I used 425gsm (200lb) Not paper, and the finished painting measures 300 x 385mm (11¾ x 15in)

You will need

Alizarin crimson, burnt umber, cadmium lemon, cerulean blue, cobalt turquoise, indigo, Naples yellow, Payne's gray, phthalo blue, phthalo green

Candle, gum arabic, masking fluid

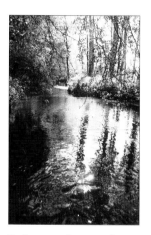

Reference photograph.

1. Mask the edges of the painting area, then draw the basic outlines of the trees on to the paper. Use an old brush to apply masking fluid to the highlight on the distant stretch of water, then use an old toothbrush to spatter random marks on the foliage and the rippled surface of the water.

Make big marks by tapping the loaded toothbrush on your hand, and small ones by scraping your finger across the bristles of the toothbrush.

2. Mask the water area of the painting with scrap paper, then use the spattering technique (see page 20) to wet the tree area. Spatter cadmium lemon to create the indication of foliage. Add Naples yellow to the mix, then brush this into the bright centre area. Use water to dilute the edges of yellow. Paint in the tree trunks with cadmium lemon. Leave to dry.

3. Use the spattering technique of wetting, painting and drying to continue building up the foliage colour by colour. Mix pale greens from cadmium yellow and phthalo green, add burnt umber to the mix on the palette for mid greens, then Payne's gray and cobalt turquoise for darker tones. Add touches of cobalt turquoise and alizarin crimson, wet into wet, into areas of yellow to define dark distant foliage behind tree trunks. Leave to dry.

4. Add more Payne's gray to green mix, then work up dark areas in the foliage at the left-hand side and along the far bank of the river. Leave to dry.

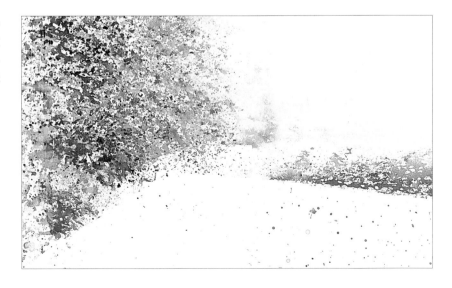

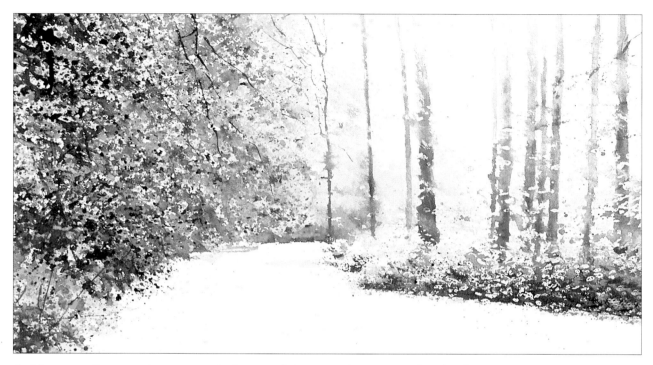

5. Use a candle to apply a wax resist here and there on the tree trunks. Apply patches of the last mix on the tree trunks, then leave to dry. Spatter water over the trees, then spatter darks into this area. Mix Naples yellow and cerulean blue, then paint the tree trunks from the bottom upwards, diluting the mix with water as you work up the trunk. Add touches of burnt umber here and there, and darken the base of the trees with Payne's gray. Add traces of branches and twigs among the splattered leaves, and a few fine branches across the tree trunks.

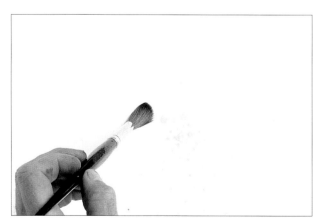

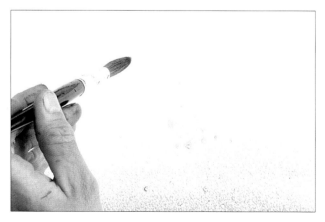

6. Now start to work on the water. At this stage treat the water as an upside-down sky, so dampen the area with water from the bottom upwards. You may note that before starting this stage, I added a few more highlights in the foreground ripples. Leave the masking fluid to dry before wetting the paper.

7. Mix a strong wash of phthalo blue, then apply it to the damp paper. Start at the bottom, then gradually weaken the wash with water as you work up the painting.

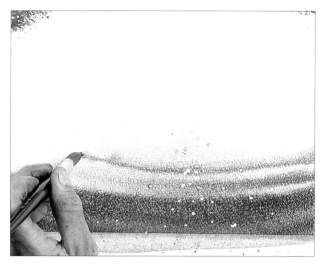

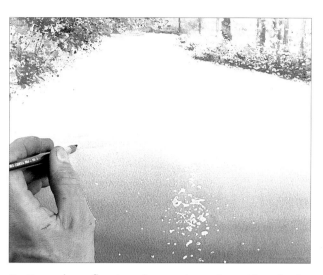

8. While the phthalo blue is still wet, lay in a graded wash of indigo, working from the bottom upwards and taking this colour just short of the weakest part of the previous phthalo blue wash. Strengthen with more colour at the bottom if necessary, then leave to dry. Indigo tends to dry much paler than it appears when wet, so apply another indigo wash if necessary.

9. Start the reflections by wetting a broad band of the water, excluding the far reach of water, then add a few streaks of gum arabic. Refer to the photographs below, at steps 10 and 11, to see the extent of the area to be wetted.

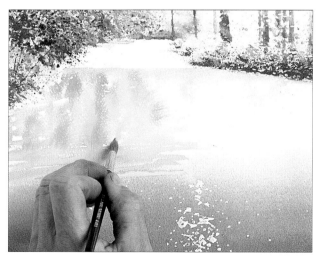

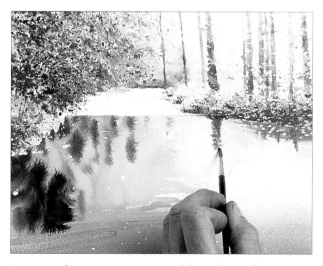

10. Work the reflections from the palest colours through to the darkest, bearing in mind that these are slightly darker than the tones they reflect due to the darkness of the river bed. Start by adding a touch of burnt sienna to cadmium lemon, then apply this colour to indicate the massed reflections of foliage. Drag the wash down to end with a broken line of horizontal ripples. Add touches of phthalo green, wet-into-wet, to indicate shadows.

11. Working wet into wet, add touches of burnt umber to Naples yellow then paint the reflections under the tree trunks. Add touches of Payne's gray to create more dark tones, and patches of cadmium lemon to give soft-edged reflection.

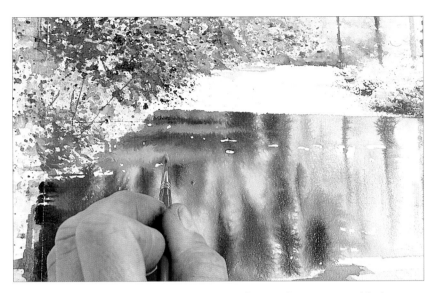

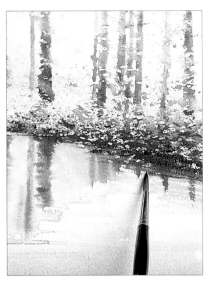

12. Add touches of cerulean blue to reflect soft passages of light passing through the canopy of trees, mixing and blending colours on the paper. Mix a dense wash cadmium lemon and burnt sienna, then add a streak of this colour to indicate a patch of sunlight on the water.

13. Use a dry brush to paint horizontal streaks of dark across the vertical reflections, leaving speckles of white paper to indicate highlights.

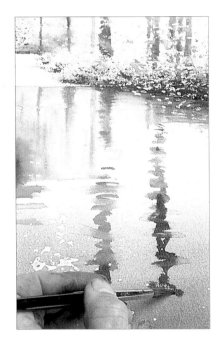

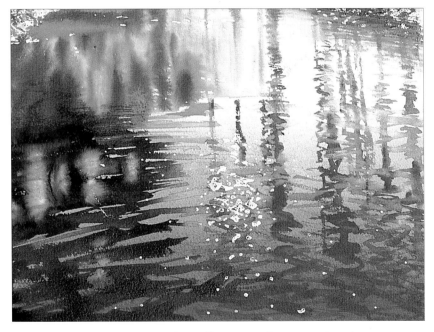

14. Use water to make crisscross reflections of the tree trunks down into the blue area of water. Use a mix of Payne's gray and the dark green on the palette to create rippled reflections.

15. Continue working up the reflections of tree trunks, then, using bold strokes, paint in the darks at the bottom left-hand corner. Add touches of cadmium lemon, wet-into-wet, to achieve a mix of hard- and soft-edged reflections.

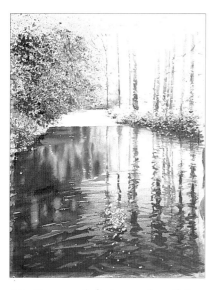

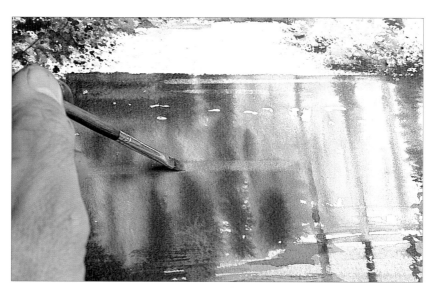

16. Start re-defining and unifying the structure of the reflection. Remember that the brushstrokes in the foreground must be larger than those in the distance.

17. Use a small bristle brush and water to leach out a few horizontal streaks across the surface of the water.

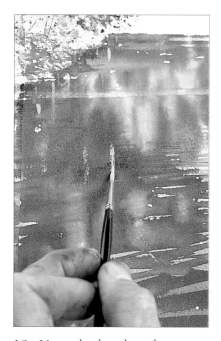

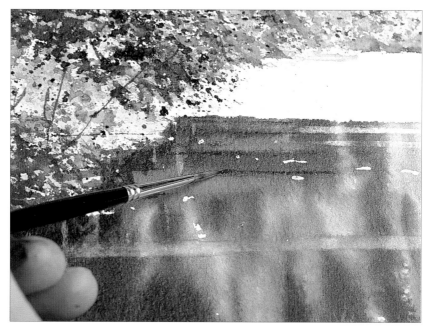

18. Use a dry brush and neat cadmium lemon to create short vertical streaks of colour to represent the strong reflections of sunlit leaves.

19. Add a few fine horizontal streaks of dark colour.

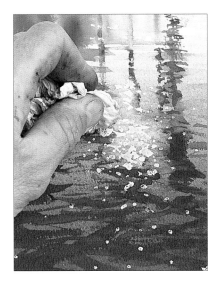

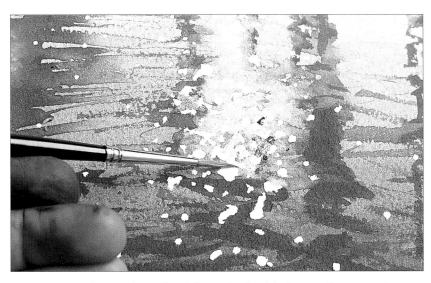

20. Use the bristle brush to scrub water around the mass of masking fluid highlights, then use a paper towel to dab off some of the colour.

21. Remove the masking fluid from the highlights in the water then start to 'model' the highlights. Break the larger marks into smaller ones by painting over them or by wetting the paper around each shape and gently dragging the surrounding colour on to them.

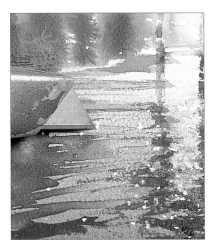

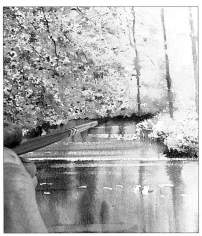

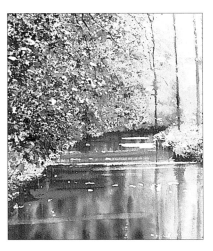

22. Re-define the reflections of tree trunk that pass through the highlights, then continue to model the highlights. Use a craft knife to scratch some of them into short vertical shapes.

23. Now block in the distant stretch of water, laying bands of cerulean blue and cadmium lemon. Add vertical streaks of yellow, then touches of Payne's gray. Define the distant river bank with a hard edge and its reflections with soft edges.

24. Finally, remove the masking fluid from the foliage and from the distant stretch of water.

Opposite
The finished painting
I added a few fine details and softened some of the exposed highlights with touches of colour.

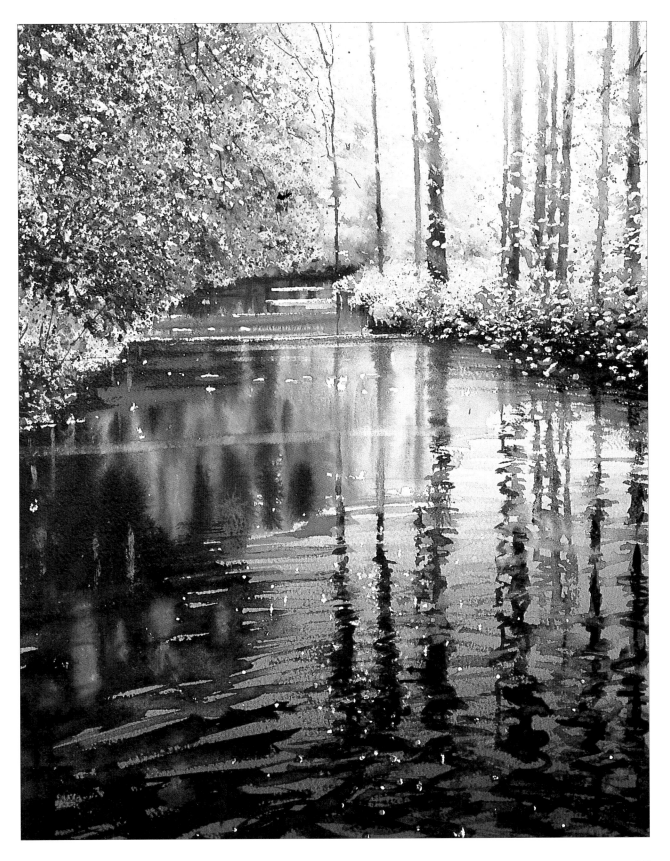

Boating Lake

The lively dance of light on the surface of the water in this painting is captured with the point of a rhythmically-worked brush before new colours – yellows, greens and browns – are sunk into the still-wet wash. Sitting just below the horizon line, the far shore is high enough to put emphasis on the foreground water, and to place the observer in the scene.

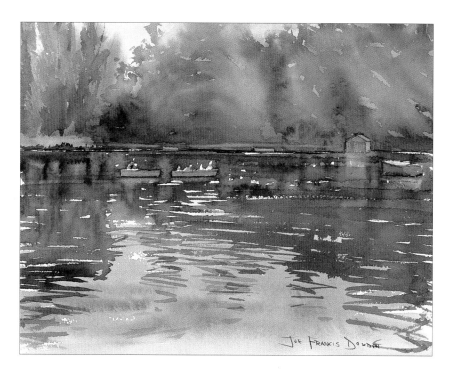

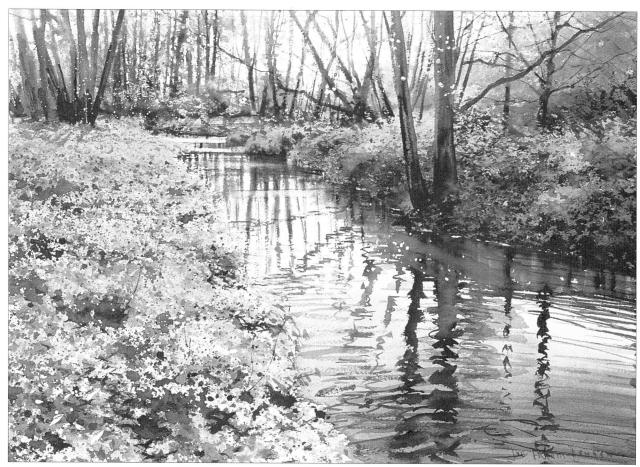

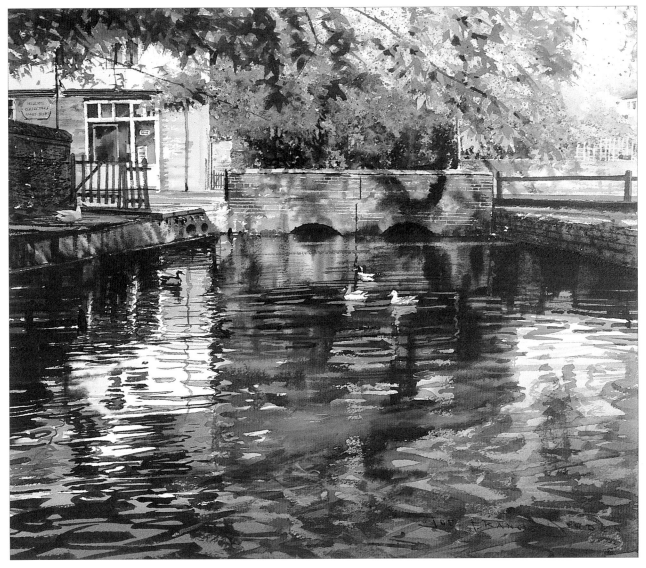

River and Road

An ancient route crosses a river at the site of a medieval village. Where they meet, the river spills out into these sunlit shallows. Rich in colour and tone, the water was worked very strongly, wet into wet. When these first colours were dry, more ripples were added, wet on dry, painting lighter opaque colours on top of the darks, much as with oil painting. The warmth of the bridge contrasts with the deep blue reflection of the sky, which is much darker than the sky itself; this is often the case with shallow water where the dark bottom enhances the darker reflections but not the lighter ones. Tonal contrast is provided by the white on the building, so the painting contains a full range of colour and tone. As well as depicting light and shade, a painting can capture the movement of water in a way that is quite unobtainable photographically. Adding water to a composition gives the artist an opportunity to bring a painting to life.

This composition was painted in the late afternoon, with the sun behind me. Compare it with the same scene shown on the front cover of this book, which was painted early in the morning, looking straight into the sun. They are as different as separate locations might be, and both were a sheer delight to paint.

Opposite

Bourneside

This rural reach, with its gently-rippled surface, agitated by a succession of small waterfalls is just what artist's brushes were made for. The point of a round sable brush effortlessly produces wave and ripple shapes as revealed by the dark reflections. The light patterns in the bed of the river, made by the flow of water, can be rendered either by lifting out colour or by dropping in semi-opaque colours – cadmium lemon, Naples yellow, Chinese white or titanium white – wet into wet.

39

Shallow water

The river depicted in this demonstration flows down from the high Andalusian mountains in Spain and forged this rocky terrain during the rainy seasons. When the waters subside, the river provides the perfect foil for this arid landscape; a deep blue sky reflecting in stretches of shallow water, rocks above and below the surface, and soft reflections from the far shore. In this painting, which measures 420 x 315mm (12½ x 16½in) and is painted on 300gsm (140lb) Not paper, I show how easy it can be to capture these features in watercolour.

You will need

Alizarin crimson, burnt sienna, burnt umber, cadmium lemon, cadmium orange, cobalt blue, cobalt turquoise, helio turquoise, indigo, Naples yellow, olive green, Payne's gray, phthalo blue, phthalo green, quinacridone red, ultramarine, yellow ochre

Masking fluid, gum arabic

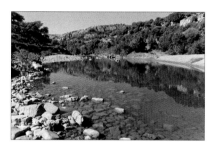

Reference photograph.

1. Tape up the outer edges of the composition, then, using the reference photograph as a guide, make a pencil sketch in the main outlines of the scene.

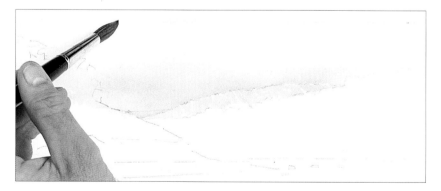

2. Wet the sky area, then lay in a graded wash of quinacridone red, from the bottom of the sky upwards over half the sky. Drag some colour down on to the hills. Leave to dry. Wet all the sky area avoiding the hills, then lay in a wash of phthalo blue with touches of helio turquoise and cobalt blue from the top of the painting downwards.

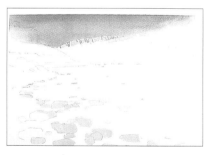

3. Strengthen the sky with cobalt blue, then add shadows in the far hills. Remove the masking tape from round the sky then, while the sky dries, use an old brush to apply masking fluid to all the dry parts of the rocks in the water.

4. Mix ultramarine with touches of quinacridone red and yellow ochre, then block in the distant horizon and add texture to the far hills. Mix yellow ochre with a touch of cadmium orange, then block in the near hills; take this colour up on to the blue at the right-hand side to create a green tree line. Use the same colour with a dry brush to indicate foliage for the trees at the left-hand side. Leave to dry.

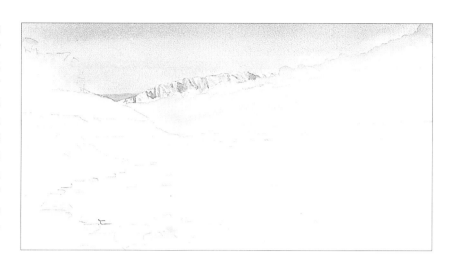

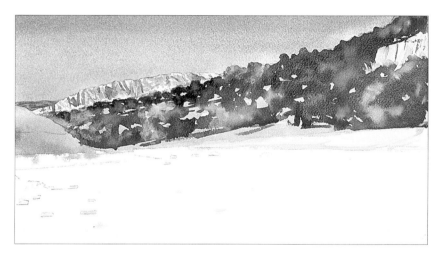

5. Glaze tones of cadmium orange and burnt umber over parts of the near hills. Dry the far bank of the river, wet the hill side, then drop in splashes of olive green, wet-into-wet, to indicate trees. Create highlights of cobalt turquoise, Naples yellow and cadmium lemon, all wet-into-wet. Create shadows with burnt umber and ultramarine. Use a clean paper towel to dab out some of the colour in the distance.

6. Wet the left-hand hill and work olive green into this area to denote foliage. Dry brush some of this colour for the trees on the skyline. Add burnt umber and ultramarine for the darks in the foliage. Add more shadows to the distant mountains and some tiny clumps of foliage on the skyline.

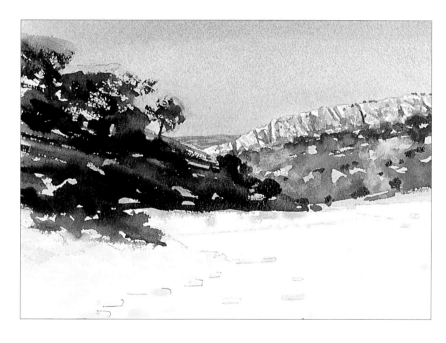

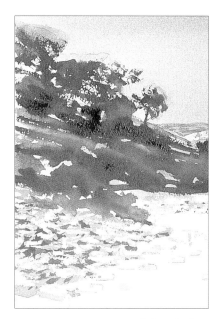

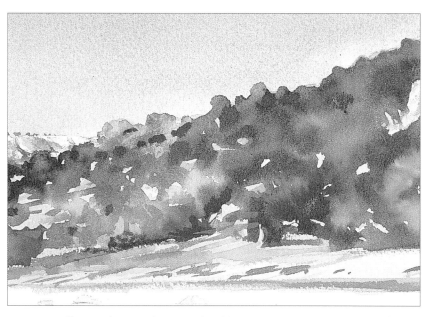

7. Using a mixture of the darks on the palette and a dry brush, crisscross texture across the rocky scree in the foreground and middle distance. Leave to dry, then crisscross small brush strokes of darker tones over the first set of brush strokes to define form and create shadows.

8. Mix yellow ochre with a touch of burnt umber, then work a few strokes of this colour across the bank of the river. Add touches of quinacridone red, then brush some of this to the bank and one or two touches to the rocky crag at top right. Add a few marks of olive green to denote patches of grass.

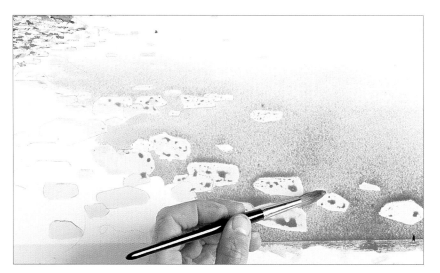

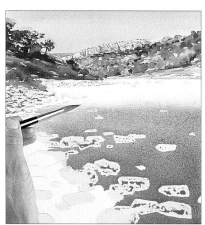

9. Wet all the water area with water, then brush gum arabic over the top 25mm (1 in) of the water. Lay a strong wash of burnt sienna across the bottom edge of the water, then, working up from the bottom, gradually dilute the wash with water.

10. Working wet into wet, add more burnt sienna to the bottom edge, then lay in neat alizarin crimson over the burnt sienna, laying a strong band of this red towards the top.

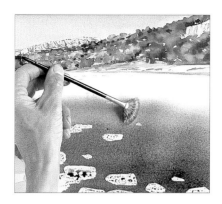

11. Working wet into wet, from the bottom upwards, lay in a wash of indigo, then add a few horizontal strokes of phthalo green. Use a dry fan brush to blend all the colours together.

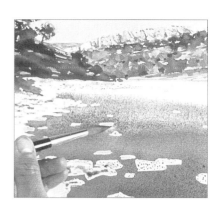

12. Mix a wash of phthalo blue, then lay a band of this colour above the red.

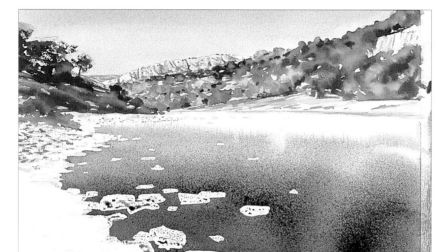

13. Bring the blue down over the previous colours, gradually diluting the wash with more water. While the blue is still wet, use a clean brush to lift out a patch of colour for the reflection of the rocky crags. Leave to dry.

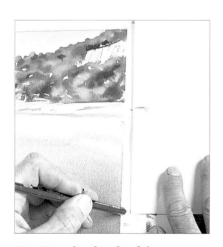

14. Size the depth of the reflection about the real horizon line. The hill at the right-hand side is cut by the top of the painting, so remember to add this missing part in the reflection.

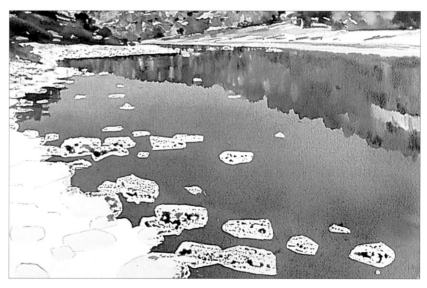

15. Wet the area of water in which the reflection of the hillside appears, then paint the reflections, wet into wet, using olive green, phthalo green, Payne's gray, cadmium orange and Naples yellow.

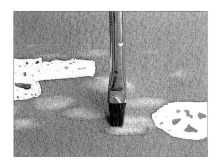

16. Use a small bristle brush to leach out patches of colour from the water to indicate the submerged rocks. Work with the board at a slight angle to allow the water to form a hard line at bottom of each rock.

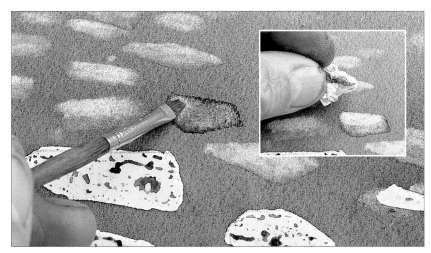

17. For the larger rocks, wet the shape of the rock with water, then use a rolled-up tissue to remove colour from the top edge of the rock.

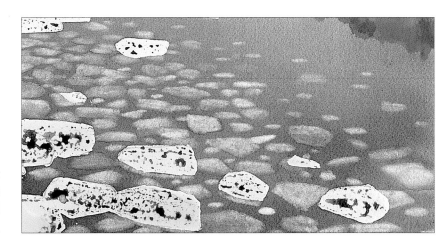

18. Continue leaching out the rest of the submerged rocks. This is very straightforward and well worth the effort.

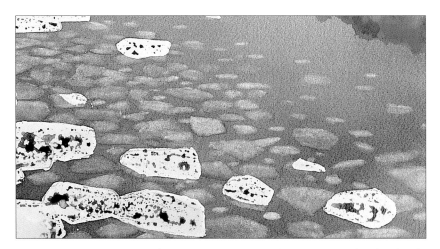

19. Use weak washes of burnt sienna to apply colour to the leached out rocks. Use paper towel to dab off excess colour from some rocks.

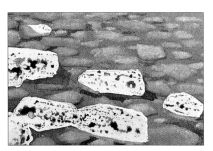

20. Use Payne's gray to add fine shadows at the right-hand and bottom sides of the large rocks. Work some wet into wet, some wet on dry. Work dark shapes between the rocks to define the underlying bed of rocks.

44

21. Remove the masking fluid, then start to colour the exposed rocks. Use mixes of burnt sienna and ultramarine, with touches of alizarin crimson here and there; make weak washes for the tops of the rocks, then strengthen the blue for the shadowed area. Use burnt umber and ultramarine for dark shadows.

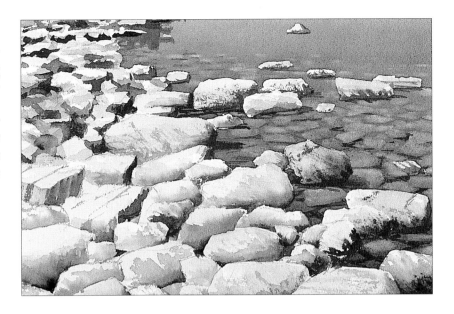

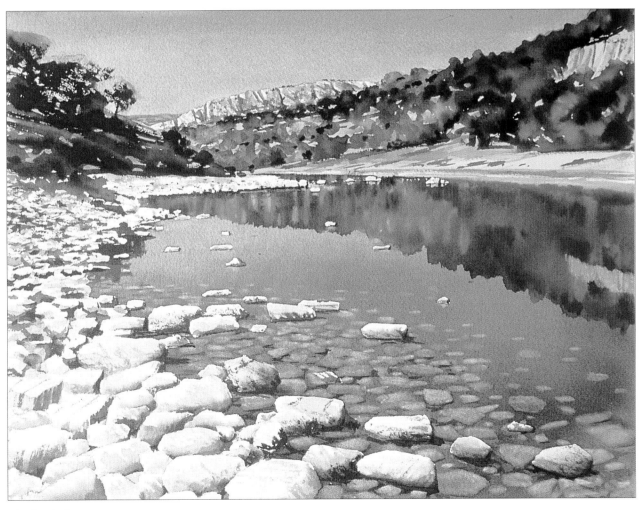

The finished painting

Sparkling Water

I painted this picture in spring, when the weather fluctuated between rain and sunshine every few minutes. The sun was directly ahead, but just above the top edge of the painting, and its intense light created the sparkling flashes of light reflected on the ripples in the water. These highlights were enhanced by the darker tones of the sombre clouds in the lower part of the sky.

This scene required strong tones in the river, and these were built up with successive glazes of Naples yellow, burnt umber and Payne's gray. The sparkles are vertical scratches, made with tip of a blade, to mimic their up and down motion in the water. In addition to these ripples, markings on the river bed are also visible. By careful observation, all these effects can be identified and painted in watercolour.

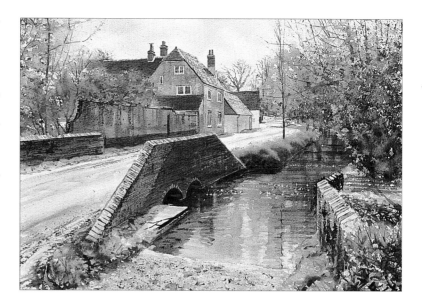

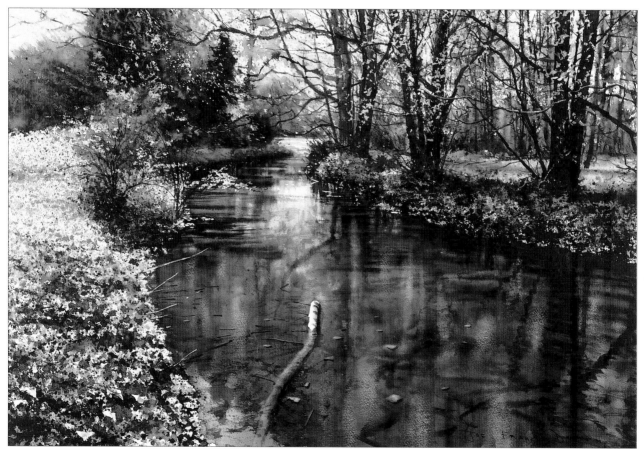

Bend in the River

The half-submerged branch was masked where it emerges from the water, and scrubbed out below the waterline. The decaying twigs and branches on the river bed were painted, wet into wet, on the strong underlying wash. The soft vertical marks are reflected highlights from the bright sky shining through the tree canopy; these were lifted out of the dry wash with a damp brush, then dabbed with a paper towel.

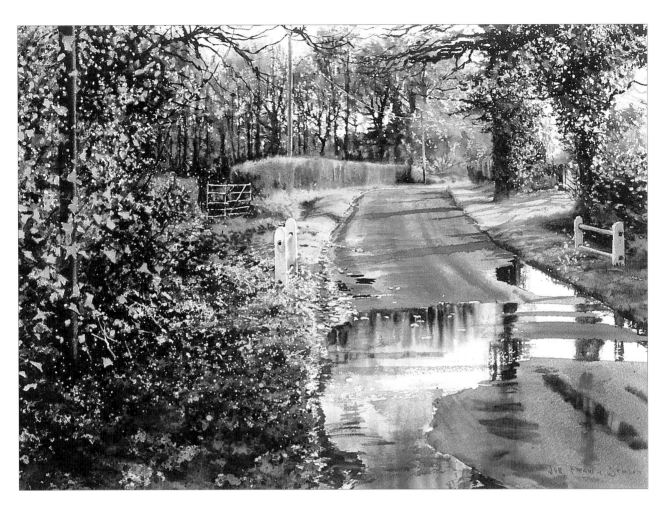

Rural Lane

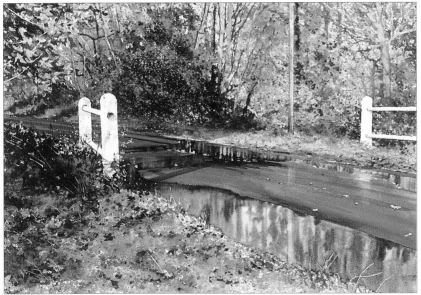

Water reflecting light is as attractive as any gem in a jeweller's shop window. Water lying on a road is often taken for granted, but reflections in the water can transform a scene and unite two halves of a composition. It is incredible how much one location can yield, and these two paintings illustrate this point. The view (left) is from the right-hand grassy bank in the painting above. Note how the telegraph pole, puddles and culvert bridge feature in each painting.

The lane is painted with ultramarine, burnt sienna and alizarin crimson; touches of cerulean blue were added to create granulation and give the tarmac texture. Gum arabic was used in the puddles, and the culvert railings were masked. Vertical reflections always help to make water look wet.

Index

Millpond and Watercourse

Although this centuries-old scene looks natural, it is man-made – a very deep millpond and a feeder stream.

I painted a deep-blue, upside-down sky wash to create the foreground stream. Then, working wet into wet, I added the dark reflections and ripples which contrast with the bright yellows and greens. Very bright colours can be used when balanced with strong dark tones. I used a different method to paint the millpond; I thoroughly wetted the area, then dropped many colours into it.

Normally, when painting water scenes, I start by working up the surrounding landscape, then use those colours for the reflections. However, when painting tree reflections, you could put these in first; without the constraints of precision, they can be completely loose and carefree. You are then at liberty to place the real trees in harmony with their reflections!

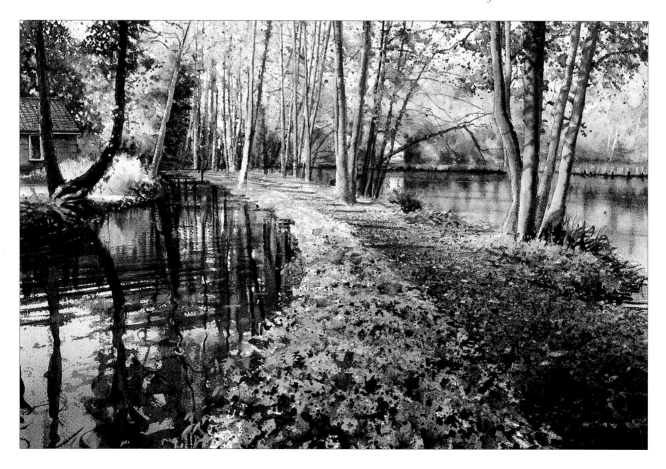